Earth Day

An Alphabet Book

Gary Kowalski

Illustrations by Rocco Baviera

Published by Skinner House Books.
Skinner House Books is an imprint of the Unitarian Universalist Association,
a liberal religious organization with more than 1,000 congregations in the U.S. and Canada.
24 Farnsworth St., Boston, MA 02210-1409

Printed in the United States.

Design and illustrations by Rocco Baviera.

ISBN: 978-1-55896-908-9

6 5 4
23 22

Library of Congress Cataloging-in-Publication Data

Kowalski, Gary A.
Earth day : an alphabet book / Gary Kowalski.
p. cm.
ISBN-13: 978-1-55896-542-3 (pbk. : alk. paper)
ISBN-10: 1-55896-542-4 (pbk. : alk. paper) 1. Nature-Prayers and
devotions-Juvenile literature. 2. English language-Alphabet-Juvenile
literature. 3. Children-Prayers and devotions. I. Title.
BL435.K69 2009
204'.32--dc22

2008019675

"Earth Day" was first published in *Green Mountain Spring and Other Leaps of Faith* by Gary A. Kowalski (Skinner House Books, 1997).

We give thanks for the earth and its creatures,
and are grateful from A to Z

Aa

For alligators, apricots, acorns, and apple trees

Bb

For bumblebees, bananas, blueberries, and beagles

Cc

Coconuts, crawdads, cornfields, and coffee

Dd Ee Ff

Daisies, elephants, and flying fish

Gg

For groundhogs, glaciers, and grasslands

Hh   Ii

Hippos and hazelnuts, icicles and iguanas

Kk   Ll

For juniper, jackrabbits, and junebugs,
Kumquats and kangaroos, lightning bugs and licorice

Mm

For mountains and milkweed and mistletoe

Nn

Narwhals and nasturtiums, otters and ocelots

Oo

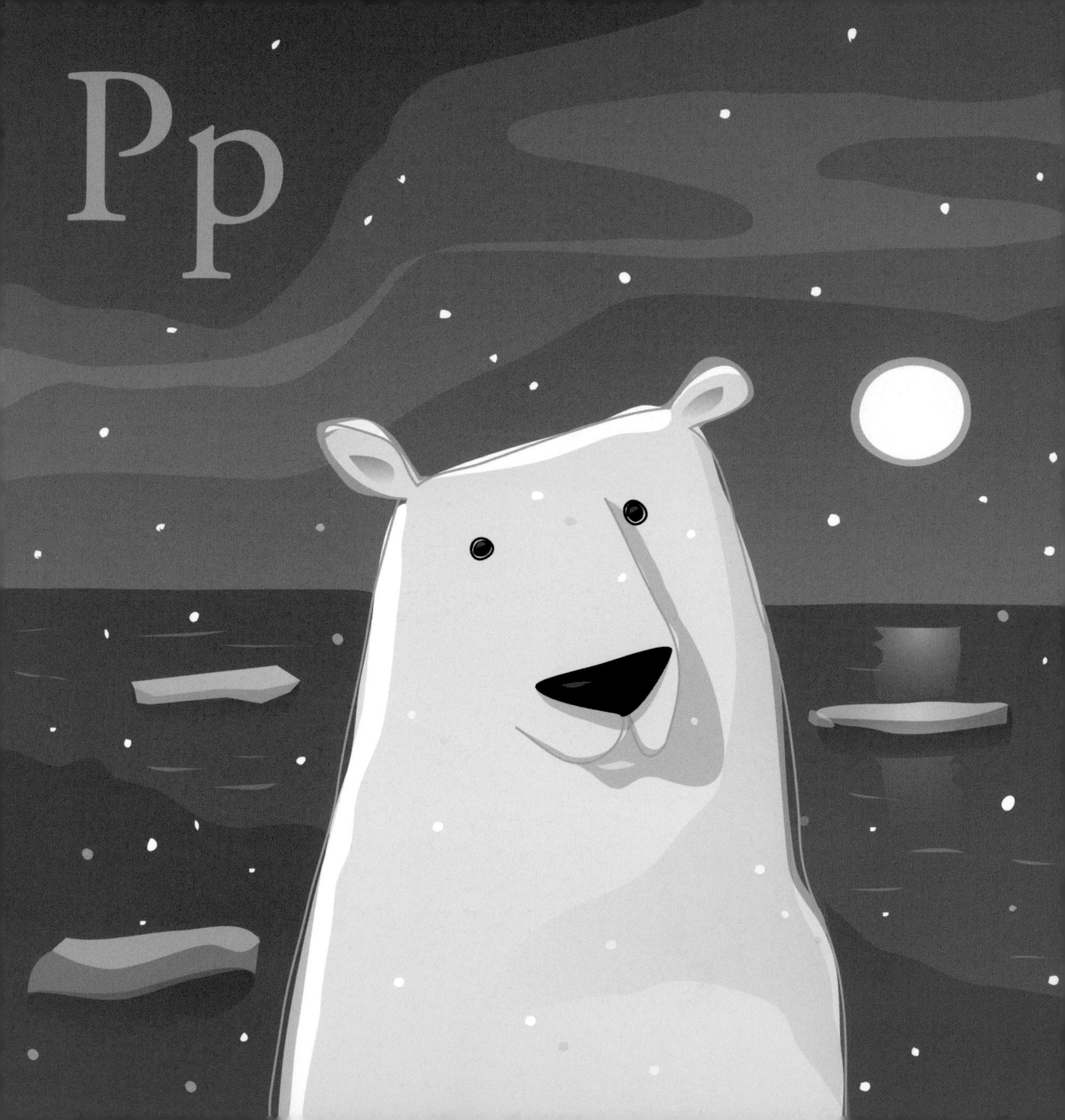
Pp

Qq

For peonies, persimmons, and polar bears,
Quahogs and Queen Anne's Lace

Rr   Ss   Tt

For raspberries and roses,
Salmon and sassafras, tornadoes and tulipwood

Uu Vv Ww

Urchins and valleys and waterfalls

For X (the unknown, the mystery of it all!)

Yy

In every yak and yam

Zz

We are grateful, good Earth, not least of all
For zinnias, zucchini, and zebras

And for the alphabet of wonderful things
that are as simple as ABC.